2.00

A Colonial Williamsburg ABC

By Amy Zakrzewski Watson

Illustrated by Louis S. Glanzman

The Colonial Williamsburg Foundation
Williamsburg, Virginia

© 1994 by The Colonial Williamsburg Foundation
All rights reserved

Artwork © 1994 by Louis S. Glanzman
ISBN 0-87935-127-6   Printed in Singapore

A a

The blacksmith works at his **anvil.**

Sparrows live in a bird bottle.

Bb

Cc

The soldier fires a **cannon.**

The man beats a **drum**.

Dd

Ee

Children gather **eggs.**

Flowers grow in a garden.

Ff

Gg

Please close the gate.

The boy rolls a **hoop.**

Hh

Ii

Thomas Jefferson uses an **inkwell**.

The fiddler plays a **jig**. Jj

Kk

Girls and boys fly **kites.**

The **lantern** lights the way. Ll

Mm

The girl wears a **mobcap.**

Mother and daughter do **needlework**.

Nn

Oo

The **oxen** pull a cart.

The **pot** holds soup.

P p

Qq

Men pitch **quoits**.

Children play **recorders.**

Rr

Ss

The **stocks** hold lawbreakers.

Boys spin **tops.** T t

Uu

A **unicorn** is on the Palace gate.

The boy plays his **violin.**

Vv

W w

The **windmill** grinds corn.

The man signs with an "X."

Xx

Yy

The woman spins **yarn.**

"ZZZ" **Zz**